READ MY LIPS, MAKE MY DAY, EAT QUICHE AND DIE!

Doonesbury Books by G. B. Trudeau

In Large Format

A DOONESBURY BOOK
by G. B. TRUDEAU

READ MY LIPS, MAKE MY DAY, EAT QUICHE AND DIE!

ANDREWS and McMEEL   A UNIVERSAL PRESS SYNDICATE COMPANY   KANSAS CITY • NEW YORK

ATTENTION: SCHOOLS AND BUSINESSES

Andrews and McMeel books are available at quantity discounts with bulk purchase for educational, business, or sales promotional use. For information, please write to: Special Sales Department, Andrews and McMeel, 4900 Main Street, Kansas City, Missouri 64112.

"George Bush says he hears the quiet people others don't.
I've got a friend in L.A. who hears the quiet people others don't,
and he's got to take a lot of medication."
— Albert Brooks

TOMORROW'S SCRIPT.

April 4, 1988
DROP BY MEETING WITH CABINET
Location: Cabinet Room.

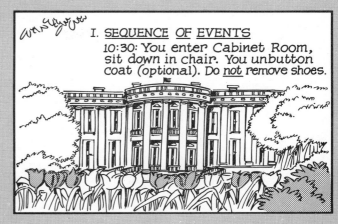

I. SEQUENCE OF EVENTS
10:30: You enter Cabinet Room, sit down in chair. You unbutton coat (optional). Do not remove shoes.

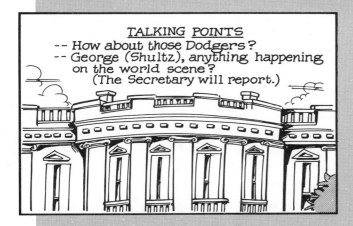

TALKING POINTS
-- How about those Dodgers?
-- George (Shultz), anything happening on the world scene?
(The Secretary will report.)

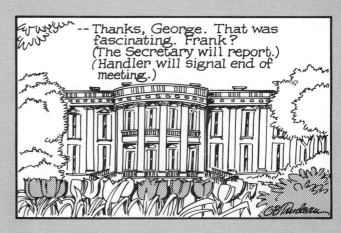

-- Thanks, George. That was fascinating. Frank?
(The Secretary will report.)
(Handler will signal end of meeting.)

10:37 a.m.: You leave Cabinet Room through same door. Return to Oval Office. Sit down.

10:40 a.m.- 6:28 p.m.: Free time.

6:30 p.m.: Meet your wife (Nancy) for dinner.
Talking points: What a day!
Is that a new dress?

10

WE'RE **BACK!** AND WHAT A GRAND FEW WEEKS IT'S BEEN FOR THE WHITE HOUSE, CAMPERS!

AS THE KISS-AND-TELL BOOKS KEEP SPEWING FORTH, IT'S HARD TO KEEP TRACK OF ALL THE NEWLY REVEALED SIDES OF THE REAGAN PERSONA!

REAGAN THE COMICS READER! REAGAN THE STAR WARRIOR! REAGAN THE ASTROLOGY BUFF! REAGAN THE SCRIPT DEVOTEE! THE BIG QUESTION: **HOW** DOES HE FIND THE TIME FOR SO MANY OUTSIDE INTERESTS?

"AVOID COMPLEX ISSUES TODAY. CONSIDER TAKING A NAP."

WHEN? NOW? BEFORE BREAKFAST?

HEY, LISTEN TO THIS, MOMMY: "MOON ASPECTS INDICATE YOU WILL BE RIDICULED TODAY FOR YOUR SUPERSTITIOUS BELIEFS"!

GEE, DO YOU THINK I SHOULD GO TO WORK?

I'M SURE IT'S OKAY, DEAR. JUST BE CAREFUL.

OH, MY GOSH...

WHAT IS IT, DEAR?

I'M IN THE COMICS!

NOW, THAT'S JUST PLAIN UNCANNY!

WHAT'S YOURS SAY, MOMMY?

OH, MY GOODNESS... LISTEN TO THIS, DEAR...

"THE MOON-VENUS CONJUNCTION REQUIRES TAKING CHARGE OF YOUR FINANCIAL AFFAIRS. NOW IS THE TIME TO SETTLE OLD DEBTS."

"P.S. MRS. R — BALANCE STILL DUE ON APRIL FORECASTS. PLEASE REMIT PROMPTLY."

WHOA...

IS THAT SPOOKY OR WHAT?

19

...AND EVEN THOUGH MOST PEOPLE THOUGHT THE QUAKE WAS DUE ON THE 23RD, NOSTRADAMUS *ACTUALLY* PREDICTED IT FOR MAY 27TH, THIS FRIDAY!

UH-HUH... WELL... THAT'S GREAT, BOOPSIE...

B.D., DIDN'T YOU HEAR ME? I SAID FRIDAY! THAT'S ONLY FOUR DAYS AWAY!

I'LL PENCIL IT IN.

B.D., THE DARN COAST IS GOING TO SLIDE INTO THE *OCEAN!*

REMIND ME TO MOVE THE CAR.

YOU SEE, B.D., NOSTRADAMUS DIDN'T PREDICT THE QUAKE FOR MAY 23. HE PREDICTED IT FOR MAY 27!

AND HOW DO YOU KNOW THIS?

WELL, IT'S A LONG STORY. I'LL TELL YOU IF YOU PROMISE NOT TO GET MAD.

YOU'RE GOING TO TELL ME WHETHER I PROMISE OR NOT, AREN'T YOU?

IN A FORMER LIFE, I USED TO DATE NOSTRADAMUS.

IMAGINE MY SURPRISE.

YOU'RE NOT JEALOUS, ARE YOU? WE ONLY WENT OUT TWICE.

HEY, BOOPSIE, IF THE EARTHQUAKE'S ON FOR FRIDAY, SHOULDN'T YOU BE PACKING?

I'M AFRAID NOT, B.D....

ACCORDING TO MY HOROSCOPE FOR FRIDAY, IT'S OUR DESTINY TO PERISH HERE IN MALIBU.

RIGHT. LEMME SEE THAT.

THERE'S NOTHING WE CAN DO ABOUT IT, B.D. QUE SERA, SERA!

"YOU AND YOUR MATE WILL DIE TAN AND RESTED."

I THINK I'LL WEAR A SHORT COCKTAIL DRESS.

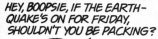

IT'S ONLY BEEN A FEW HOURS SINCE J.J. LEFT MIKE.

DING DONG!

RIGHT ON SCHEDULE...

ZONKER. WHAT A SURPRISE.

I'M HERE FOR YOU, BUDDY. HAVE I MISSED LUNCH?

CLASS OF '88, FOR FOUR YEARS, YOU HAVE LIVED IN AN ENCLAVE OF TRANQUILITY AND PRIVILEGE.

FAR FROM THE MADDING CROWD, YOU HAVE SLOWLY MARINATED YOURSELVES IN CIVILIZATION'S HIGHEST IDEALS AND VALUES.

IT IS NOW TIME FOR YOU TO EXPERIENCE LIFE AS IT REALLY IS, AND WE PRAY WE HAVE PREPARED YOU FOR IT ADEQUATELY.

IN A FEW HOURS, BEYOND THOSE GATES, YOU WILL DISCOVER A WORLD OF HURT! YOU'LL FIND A SOCIETY WHICH SIMPLY DOESN'T WORK FOR MANY OF ITS...

EXCUSE ME?

...ITS...

I HAVEN'T EATEN TODAY. COULD YOU SPARE SOMETHING?

CHINK CHINK!

NOT YET, FOR CRYING OUT LOUD!

WHAT?

YO! HOME BOY! GOT ANY SPARE CHANGE?

ARE YOU KIDDING? I OWE THIS PLACE $40,000.

GB Trudeau

AN EPIPHANY.

LOOK AT THE FACTS, SIR. THE SOVIETS ARE IN THE THROES OF PERESTROIKA, THE CHINESE ARE RESTRUCTURING **THEIR** ECONOMY...

FROM POLAND TO VIETNAM, DISCREDITED COMMUNIST ECONOMIC AND POLITICAL MODELS ARE BEING CHALLENGED, WHILE CAPITALIST VALUES ARE EMBRACED!

WHAT ARE YOU SAYING HERE, HOWARD?

I'M SAYING THE COLD WAR IS **OVER**, SIR! IT'S OVER, AND WE **WON**!

WE WON?

WITHIN HOURS, TIMES SQUARE ERUPTED.

U.S.A.!

WE'RE NUMBER ONE!

VICTORY!

COLD WAR OVER!

NEW YORK POST

COLD

THE NEWS WAS STAGGERING...

THE DAILY NEWS

COLD WAR OVER: WE WON!

WEST VICTORI IN 43-YEAR CONFLICT!

ALSO: YANKS SWEEP SOX

THOUSANDS OF JUBILANT CAPITALISTS POURED INTO TIMES SQUARE...

HELLO, EVERYBODY! I'M ROLAND HEDLEY, ALONG WITH PERSONALITY BARBARA ANN BOOPSTEIN, COMING TO YOU LIVE FROM NEW YORK CITY, WHERE A TUMULTUOUS COLD WAR **VICTORY PARADE** IS STILL IN PROGRESS!

AND HERE COMES "THE WALL STREET JOURNAL" FLOAT, BOOPSIE!

THAT'S RIGHT, ROLAND! AND LOOK! THERE'S **MALCOLM FORBES**!

HI, EVERYONE! I'M ROLAND HEDLEY, ALONG WITH BARBARA ANN BOOPSTEIN, OVERLOOKING A PACKED TIMES SQUARE COLD WAR **VICTORY CELEBRATION**!

AN ESTIMATED 600,000 JUBILANT CAPITALISTS HAVE CRAMMED THIS HISTORIC DISTRICT TO CELEBRATE THE TRIUMPH OF FREE MARKET DEMOCRACY OVER THE MORIBUND SOVIET SYSTEM!

YES, THE COLD WAR IS **OVER**! FROM THE HILLS OF AFGHANISTAN TO THE MARKETS OF SHANGHAI TO THE SHIPYARDS OF GDANSK, COMMUNISM AS WE KNOW IT IS IN FULL, OPEN RETREAT!

BUT YOU GOTTA GIVE THOSE SOVIETS CREDIT, DON'T YOU, ROLLIE?

YOU BET, BOOPSIE! THEY SHOWED A LOT OF CHARACTER, A LOT OF MENTAL TOUGHNESS!

WE'RE DOWN ON THE STREET NOW TALKING TO INDUSTRIALIST **BIG JIM ANDREWS!** ANY REACTION TO YOUR COLD WAR BLOWOUT, JIM?

HOW SWEET IT IS, ROLAND, HOW **SWEET** IT IS!

THE REDS GAVE US A REAL RUN FOR OUR MONEY, I'LL TELL YOU THAT! BUT WE BEAT THEM WITH THE BASICS: HARD CURRENCY, CHEAP WHEAT AND GOOD ROCK 'N' ROLL!

JIM'S WIFE, KATHY, IS ALSO WITH US! ANY REACTION, KATHY?

I'M JUST GLAD IT'S OVER. JIM'S BEEN A COLD WARRIOR FOR OVER 35 YEARS.

WELL, WELCOME HOME, SOLDIER! WHERE YOU HEADED?

THE SUBURBS!

WE'RE GOING TO CELEBRATE OUR WAY OF LIFE! JUST THE TWO OF US!

AS THE PANDEMONIUM CONTINUES IN TIMES SQUARE, I'M NOW TALKING TO FREE MARKETEER PHIL SLACKMEYER! PHIL, IT'S A GREAT DAY FOR WALL STREET TODAY, ISN'T IT?

YES, IT IS, AND YOU KNOW, ROLAND, IT'S ABOUT TIME! WALL STREET HAS GOTTEN RAPPED A LOT LATELY, BUT IT WAS THERE THAT THE BATTLE AGAINST THE STATE-PLANNED ECONOMY WAS WON!

SURE, SOMETIMES THE COLD WAR GOT DIRTY. SOMETIMES WE HAD TO CUT A FEW CORNERS TO MAINTAIN CASH FLOW. BUT I'D DO IT ALL OVER AGAIN, EVEN IF IT MEANT DOING MORE TIME!

HEY, THAT'S RIGHT. WHAT ARE YOU DOING OUT OF...

AMNESTY.

YOU KNOW, BOOPSIE, WE CAN TALK ABOUT THE AFGHAN REBS, WE CAN TALK ABOUT SOLIDARITY, BUT I GATHER YOU FEEL THE **REAL** COLD WAR SHOCK TROOPS HAVE BEEN WESTERN ROCKERS, RIGHT?

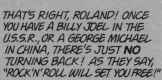

THAT'S RIGHT, ROLAND! ONCE YOU HAVE A BILLY JOEL IN THE U.S.S.R., OR A GEORGE MICHAEL IN CHINA, THERE'S JUST **NO** TURNING BACK! AS THEY SAY, "ROCK 'N' ROLL WILL SET YOU FREE!"

ROCK 'N' ROLL IS ALL **ABOUT** CHALLENGES TO AUTHORITY. SO INSTEAD OF B-1'S, WE SHOULD BE SENDING THEM **U-2!** BEFORE USING STINGERS, WE SHOULD HIT THEM WITH **STING!**

LET'S MAKE 'EM BOP 'TIL THEY **DROP!** LET'S...

EXCUSE ME, BOOPSIE! HERE COME THE MERRILL LYNCH **PRANCING BULLS!**

HI, KID.

DAD! MY GOD! WHAT ARE YOU DOING OUT?

AMNESTY! THE PRESIDENT DECLARED AN AMNESTY FOR ALL THOSE CONVICTED OF WHITE-COLLAR CRIMES DURING THE COLD WAR! I'M A FREE MAN!

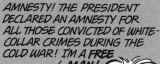

AMNESTY?

THAT'S RIGHT.

BUT THAT'S... THAT'S OUTRAGEOUS!

CAREFUL. I'M A WAR HERO NOW.

LOOK, KID, MOST OF US WERE GUILTY OF NOTHING MORE THAN CAPITALISTIC ZEAL. HELL, IT WASN'T UNTIL RECENTLY THAT INSIDER TRADING WAS EVEN CONSIDERED A CRIME!

IT WAS MEN LIKE US WHO WON THE COLD WAR! AMNESTY WAS THE LEAST WE DESERVED!

RRING!

YEAH, BUT WHAT GUARANTEE DOES SOCIETY HAVE THAT YOU GUYS WON'T STRIKE AGAIN?

HONEY? IT'S LEE'S LAWYER. HE'S BEEN CAUGHT EMBEZZLING.

SEE!

AMAZING. ZURICH HASN'T EVEN OPENED YET.

PHIL?

WHAT IS IT, MARILOU?

THE WALL STREET JOURNAL

IT'S THE WHITE HOUSE, DEAR. THEY WANT TO KNOW IF WE'LL BE ATTENDING THE WHITE-COLLAR AMNESTY BALL TOMORROW NIGHT.

TOMORROW? I DON'T KNOW, WHAT DO YOU THINK? IT'S SUCH A HASSLE GETTING DOWN THERE...

ED MEESE IS THE ENTERTAINMENT.

HMM... I DO NEED A JOB...

33

MR. PHIL SLACKMEYER, FORMERLY OF THE DANBURY CORRECTIONAL FACILITY!

GOOD EVENING, MR. PRESIDENT!

NICE TO MEET YOU, BILL.

UH... ACTUALLY, SIR, I USED TO BE ON YOUR COUNCIL OF ECONOMIC ADVISERS.

YOU DON'T SAY! AND WHAT DID YOU DO DURING THE COLD WAR?

I SCARFED UP SMALL COMPANIES, SIR.

GOOD FOR YOU! WELCOME HOME, SOLDIER!

INTERESTING PERSONAL FOOTNOTE, CAMPERS! AT THIS VERY MOMENT, MY FATHER IS ABOUT TO HAVE DINNER WITH RONALD REAGAN!

I KNOW WHAT YOU'RE ALL WONDERING: WHAT COULD MARVELOUS MARK'S OLD MAN POSSIBLY HAVE IN COMMON WITH THE PRESIDENT OF THE UNITED STATES?

DON'T ASK.

YOU WERE AT DANBURY? SOME OF MY FAVORITE AIDES WENT THERE!

YES, SIR. THEY SEND THEIR BEST.

AND IF IT WEREN'T FOR MEN LIKE YOU, THE COLD WAR WOULD HAVE PROBABLY DRAGGED ON FOR ANOTHER 20 YEARS!

HISTORY HAS ALWAYS ADVANCED IN THE WAKE OF THOSE WHO WEREN'T AFRAID TO TAKE CHANCES!

SO YOU CUT A FEW CORNERS. SO YOU BENT A FEW RULES. SO YOU ACCUMULATED A FEW FELONY COUNTS ALONG THE WAY. IS THAT REALLY SO BAD?

YOU KNOW, MEESE IS THE FIRST ATTORNEY GENERAL I'VE EVER REALLY BEEN ABLE TO RELATE TO.

ME, TOO. HE'S SO HUMAN.

CLAP! CLAP. CLAP. CLAP! CLAP! CLAP!

SKULL AND BONES. THE YALE SE-CRET SOCIETY SO SACRED IT DARES NOT BREATHE ITS OWN NAME.

DEEP IN THE INNER SANCTUM OF THE SOCIETY'S WINDOWLESS MAUS-OLEUM, A 40TH REUNION OF BONESMEN WAS IN PROGRESS...

322

THE CREAM OF THE CLASS OF '48 HAD ASSEMBLED FOR AN EVENING OF RITUAL AND REMINISCENCE.

FOR GEORGE BUSH, IT WAS A HOMECOMING.

SO! POPPY! WHAT HAVE YOU BEEN DOING?

UM... RUNNING FOR PRESI-DENT.

SKULL AND BONES: SANCTUARY TO GEORGE "POPPY" BUSH AND 14 OTHER STALWARTS FROM YALE'S CLASS OF '48.

322

HERE HAD BEEN FORGED THOSE VERY QUALITIES THAT HAD BROUGHT POPPY SO FAR: HIS ABIDING SENSE OF HONOR...

I WOULD SOONER DIE THAN REVEAL OUR SA-CRED NUMBER, 322!

...HIS ABILITY TO KEEP A SECRET...

WHAT WAS THAT NUMBER AGAIN?...

...AND, OF COURSE, HIS LEG-ENDARY POLITICAL COURAGE.

OKAY, THE VOTE IS NOW 7 TO 7! POPPY?

UM... I'LL ABSTAIN.

FOR "POPPY" BUSH AND HIS PEERS, THE BONES EX-PERIENCE WAS SEMINAL...

WOW...

...FOR AT THE CORE OF THE SO-CIETY'S MYSTIQUE WAS ITS EM-PHASIS ON MALE BONDING.

FELLOWS, WHAT SAY WE ALL POP DOWN TO THE STORK CLUB? SANS GIRLFRIENDS, OF COURSE!

MEMBERS WERE EXPECTED TO REVEAL THEIR INNERMOST SELVES, SPIRITUAL, INTELLECTUAL...

BUT WAS KANT SPEAKING TO ME? I COULDN'T TELL!

...AND, OF COURSE, PSYCHOSEXUAL.

...AND BEFORE I KNEW IT, I WAS GETTING SERIOUS FIRST-BASE ACTION!

GET OUTA HERE!

ON HORSE-BACK?

FOR BONESMEN LIKE POPPY, TRADITION RAN DEEP. THERE WAS THE EXQUISITE SUSPENSE OF "TAP"...

SKULL AND BONES! ACCEPT OR REJECT!

ACCEPT! GOD, I ACCEPT!

TAP! TAP!

...THE KINSHIP AND BONDING WITH ILLUSTRIOUS ALUMNI...

...AND THE CONVIVIAL, RITUALISTIC TOASTING IN LONG-DEAD TONGUES.

EGO! ERGO, EGO!

IBID!

OH, AND THE NUDE WRESTLING.

GIVE ME YOUR BEST SHOT, POPPY!

DEEP DOO-DOO CITY...

NEEDLESS TO SAY, POPPY WAS THE PRIDE OF THE BONES CLASS OF '48.

THE NOMINEE? REALLY? WHICH PARTY?

THAT EVENING, THE BONESMEN REMINISCED ABOUT THOSE LONG-AGO INCIDENTS WHICH BESPOKE FUTURE GREATNESS FOR POPPY...

OH, SURE, I KNEW. EVEN THEN I KNEW!

HOW? HOW'D YOU KNOW?

UH...WELL, UH... IT WAS NOTHING SPECIFIC YOU DID... JUST A...UH... FEELING...

I RECALL SOMETHING. ONE TIME, YOU...YOU...

YES?

NO, NO... THAT WAS SOMEONE ELSE...

ARE YOU SURE YOU WERE IN OUR CLASS, POPPY?

AS DAWN BROKE OVER NEW HAVEN, THE BONESMEN BID GOOD LUCK TO THEIR COMRADE WHO WOULD BE PRESIDENT...

GIVE 'EM HECK, POPPY!

THANKS, GUYS.

BY THE WAY, POPPY, WHAT'S THIS MAN DUKAKIS LIKE, ANYWAY?

HE'S A HARVARD BOUTIQUE LIBERAL.

NINE MILLION DOLLARS WAS QUICKLY RAISED.

...AND I'LL HAVE ALL MY PEOPLE GIVE THE LIMIT!

YOU FELLOWS ARE THE BEST!

YOU REALLY THINK HUNK-RA AND I ARE ON TO SOME-THING, SID?

ARE YOU SERIOUS, KID? ARE YOU FOR **REAL**?

YOUR TREATMENT IS A **CLASSIC!** YOU TWO ARE GOING TO BE A MA-JOR, **MAJOR** CREATIVE FORCE IN THIS TOWN!

LET'S TALK TICKET! TELL ME WHAT YOU WANT, BABE! HOW DO YOU WANT ME TO STRUC-TURE YOUR DEAL?

I DON'T KNOW. WHAT-EVER SEEMS...

HUNK WANT GROSS PROFIT POSITION!

ONE AT A TIME, KIDS.

©BTrudeau

YOU WANT ELEMENTS, NED? I GOT ELEMENTS OUT THE **WAZOO!** FOR LEAD, I'VE GOT EDDIE MUR-PHY AS A **MAJOR** MAYBE! FOR DIRECTOR, I'M ON SPIELBERG'S SHORT LIST OF CALLS HE'S RETURNING!

AND FOR CONCEPT, I'VE GOT A HOT NEW SPIRITUAL MOVEMENT! THE MOVIE'LL BE THE VISUAL EQUIVA-LENT OF NEW AGE MUSIC: HIP, NON-INTRUSIVE, HYPNOTIC...

...AND BEST OF ALL, YOU CAN EXPERIENCE IT OVER AND OVER AGAIN WITHOUT REMEMBERING ANYTHING!

PASS. IT'S BEEN DONE.

IT'S BEEN DONE?

IT'S CALLED TELEVISION. WHAT ELSE YOU GOT?

©BTrudeau

OKAY, LET'S SEE... NEXT, OUR HEROINE, CRYSTAL, MEETS A PSYCHIC HEALER, RANDY, WHO INTRODUCES HER TO HER DI-VINE SPARK, VIOLA.

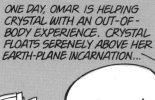

ONE DAY, OMAR IS HELPING CRYSTAL WITH AN OUT-OF-BODY EXPERIENCE. CRYSTAL FLOATS SERENELY ABOVE HER EARTH-PLANE INCARNATION...

¿SNARF!¿ SUD-DENLY, OMAR'S BROADSWORD SLICES OPEN CRYSTAL'S HEAD LIKE AN **EGG-PLANT!**

HUNK! CUT IT OUT!

CREATIVE DIFFER-ENCES?

HUNK KEEPS TRYING TO MAKE IT MORE COM-MERCIAL!

©BTrudeau

OKAY, THE SPOT OPENS WITH A GUY WAKING UP IN HIS BED...

MORNING

HE LOOKS AROUND. DISASTER! HIS WIFE HAS PACKED UP AND LEFT HIM IN THE MIDDLE OF THE NIGHT!

GONE

HE'S DESPONDENT. HE SPENDS ALL DAY LOOKING OUT THE WINDOW, BROODING ABOUT HIS LIFE...

MORNING GO

FINALLY, HE GOES TO THE REFRIGERATOR, OPENS IT, AND SEES THE PRODUCT. HE CHUGS DOWN ONE CAN AND OPENS ANOTHER.

DRINKS THE BEER.

HE'S FEELING BETTER. LIFE COULD BE WORSE. HE FLIPS THROUGH HIS TELEPHONE BOOK AND CALLS UP AN OLD GIRLFRIEND...

"HELLO, TIFFANY..."

©B Trudeau

FADE TO BLACK.

MIKE, IS EVERYTHING OKAY AT HOME?

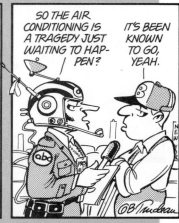

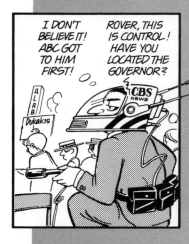

IN THE VIEW OF SOME OBSERVERS, THE ANNOUNCEMENT WAS LONG OVERDUE...

OKAY, OKAY, I CAN TAKE A HINT, HINT!

THE VOTERS HAVE SPOKEN! AND WHAT DID THESE GENIUSES SAY? "LET GEORGE DO IT, DO IT!"

SO BE IT! TODAY I AM F-F-FORMALLY WITHDRAWING AS A CANDIDATE FOR THE G.O.P. NOMINATION...

AM I TEED OFF? BITTER? HEY, WHO WOULDN'T BE? I GAVE THE MEDIA GREAT PICTURE! I GAVE THEM EVEN BETTER SOUND BITE! THEY GAVE ME D-D-DIDDLY SQUAT, SQUAT!

WELL, THEY WON'T HAVE RON HEADREST TO FLIP OFF ANYMORE! I HOPE YOU'RE... ⸘SOB! S-S-SATISFIED!

IN KENNEBUNK-PORT, THERE WAS JOY.

AT LAST! I'M FINALLY RID OF THAT...

WRONG, WIMPBURGER! I'M BACK! I JUST WENT INTO RE-RE-RE-RUNS!

44

Row 1, Panel 1: **OFF ATLANTIC CITY, ABOARD THE "TRUMP PRINCESS"...**

Row 1, Panel 2: **...DONALD TRUMP'S NEW $37 MILLION FLOATING PLAYPEN...**

Row 1, Panel 3: **...WHERE THE BATHROOM FIXTURES ARE GOLD, AND EACH OF THE 11 SUITES HAS CHAMOIS WALLS.**

Row 1, Panel 4: **...A NEW CAPTAIN IS BEING HIRED.**

AND YOU SAY YOU'RE DISCREET?

I'M YOUR MAN, MR. TRUMP!

Row 2, Panel 1: AND THIS IS MY PRIVATE SUN DECK! IT HAS BULLET-PROOF GLASS, A CIRCULAR POOL, AND A HYDRAULICALLY LIFTED SUN BED!

AMAZING, MR. TRUMP!

Row 2, Panel 2: QUALITY MEANS EVERYTHING, CAPTAIN! THE TORTOISE SHELL CEILING! IT'S UNBELIEVABLE THIS MUCH QUALITY EXISTS OUTSIDE MY IMAGINATION!

Row 2, Panel 3: AND LOOK, MORE QUALITY! THE ONYX DESK, HAND CARVED BY A WHOLE VILLAGE OF ARTISANS!

INCREDIBLE!

Row 2, Panel 4: AND OVER THERE, THAT'S MY WIFE! **LOOK** AT THE QUALITY!

VERY IMPRESSIVE!

Row 3, Panel 1: LOOK AT THE QUALITY! CHAMOIS LEATHER WALLS! BIRD'S-EYE MAPLE TRIM! HAND-CARVED ONYX BATHROOMS! WE'RE TALKING **QUALITY!** A LEVEL OF QUALITY THAT'S HARD TO EXPLAIN!

TRUMP PRINCES

Row 3, Panel 2: LOOK HERE, **MORE** QUALITY...

EXCUSE ME, SIR. BY "QUALITY", YOU MEAN IT **COSTS** AN OBSCENE AMOUNT, RIGHT?

UH... RIGHT.

Row 3, Panel 3: THERE ARE OTHER DEFINITIONS?

NONE THAT MATTER. I WAS JUST CHECKING.

YES, MR. TRUMP?

FIRE HER UP, CAPTAIN. I WANT YOU TO TAKE HER TO NEW ORLEANS!

NEW ORLEANS, SIR?

THE G.O.P. CONVENTION— WHERE THE ACTION IS! HAVE OUR ON-BOARD PUBLICIST GET ON IT!

BY SHOWING UP IN THE "TRUMP PRINCESS," WE CAN SEND AMERICA AN IMPORTANT MESSAGE ABOUT THE LAST EIGHT YEARS!

WHICH MESSAGE IS THAT, SIR?

TAX BREAKS FOR THE RICH WORK!

A GOOD MESSAGE, SIR! A TIMELY MESSAGE!

LADIES AND GENTLEMEN, BEFORE WE SET SAIL FOR NEW ORLEANS, A FEW WORDS ABOUT CREW DISCIPLINE!

THIS IS A TRUMP BOAT, AND LIKE ANY OTHER TRUMP OPERATION, IT SHALL BE RUN WITH A GLEAMING, STAINLESS STEEL FIST!

TO DEMONSTRATE HOW TOTAL MY AUTHORITY IS, I'VE DECIDED, IN HONOR OF MRS. TRUMP, TO FIRE EVERYONE WHOSE NAME BEGINS WITH "I"!

DUKEY... NO!

UH... EXCEPT FOR MISS IVEY, MY CABIN BOY.

...AND WHILE EVERYONE ELSE WAS WAITING FOR THE PRICE TO GO DOWN, I STEPPED IN WITH $30 MILLION CASH AND SNAPPED UP A BOAT WHOSE REPLACEMENT VALUE IS $180 MILLION!

IT WAS A NEGOTIATING TRIUMPH! THE "TRUMP PRINCESS" IS A FLOATING TRIBUTE TO THE ART OF MAKING A DEAL!

HEE, HEE!

WHAT'S SO FUNNY, CAPTAIN?

NOTHING'S FUNNY, SIR. I JUST **LOVE** THAT YOU CALL DEAL-MAKING AN "ART."

CLASSY, HUH? IT WAS MY WIFE'S IDEA.

IT REALLY PUTS PAINTING AND LITERATURE IN THEIR PLACE.

MAN, YOU MUST **REALLY** LOVE BOATS TO PICK UP THIS BEHEMOTH, MR. T!

ARE YOU KIDDING? I **HATE** BOATS! I ONLY CARE ABOUT CREATING AN IMPRESSION.

YOU WANT TO CREATE AN IMPRESSION, SIR? BLOW THE SUCKER UP. **THAT** WOULD CREATE AN IMPRESSION! AND SINCE ITS REPLACEMENT VALUE IS $180 MILLION, YOU COULD CLEAR $150 MILLION PROFIT IN INSURANCE!

OKAY, THAT'S ILLEGAL, BUT I LIKE YOU.

YES, SIR. I CAN'T TELL YOU HOW MANY PEOPLE HAVE TOLD ME WE DESERVE EACH OTHER.

I GUESS COMING DOWN HERE WAS A GOOD IDEA, MR. TRUMP! LOOK AT THE RECEPTION YOU'RE GETTING!

WELL, OF COURSE, CAPTAIN! WHETHER IN ATLANTIC CITY OR NEW ORLEANS, THERE WILL **ALWAYS** BE AN AUDIENCE FOR QUALITY!

THESE ARE MY PEOPLE, CAPTAIN, THE STRIVERS, THE WANNA-BES, THE LITTLE PEOPLE WITH BIG DREAMS!

YOO-HOO! DONALD! OVER **HERE**!

WARNING!

YOU SEEN THE VICE PRESIDENT, SENATOR?

NO, HE DIDN'T MAKE IT. FROM WHAT I HEAR, HIS HANDLERS ARE KEEPING HIM UNDER WRAPS UNTIL TOMORROW.

THEY FIGURE REAGAN'S RECEPTION IN THE BOWL TONIGHT COULD PROVE EMBARRASSING.

EMBARRASSING? THAT'S PUTTING IT MILDLY.

FOUR MORE YEARS! FOUR MORE YEARS!

SIGH...

DON'T BE FOOLED BY DUKAKIS' SELF-SERVING DISAVOWAL OF POLITICAL LABELS! THIS MAN IS A SNARLING, RAVING LIBERAL!

IF IT LOOKS LIKE A LIBERAL, ACTS LIKE A LIBERAL, AND SPENDS LIKE A LIBERAL, THE ODDS ARE PRETTY GOOD THAT IT'S A LIBERAL!

BE FOREWARNED, AMERICA! MICHAEL DUKAKIS IS NOW AND ALWAYS HAS BEEN, A CARD-CARRYING LIBERAL!

BOOGA! BOOGA! BOOGA!

THIS IS IRRESPONSIBLE! THERE ARE CHILDREN STILL UP AT THIS HOUR!

CHATTER! CHATTER!

IS THE BUSHMAN ON YET?

IN A MOMENT...

HIS SON IS INTRODUCING HIM NOW.

HIS SON MADE A VIDEO?

IT'S NOT A VIDEO. IT'S A SLIDE SHOW.

SLIDE SHOW?

NEXT, PLEASE. OKAY, THIS IS MY DAD'S 25-YEAR-OLD GOLF CART...

GOVERNOR DUKAKIS SAYS THE ELECTION IS ABOUT COMPETENCE. WELL, IT'S NOT! IT'S ABOUT IDEOLOGY! I WANT THE ELECTION TO BE ABOUT IDEOLOGY BECAUSE **HE'S** A LIBERAL!

YOU REMEMBER LIBERALS, DON'T YOU? LIBERALS GAVE US... GAVE US... UH...

MY GOD... WHAT HAPPENED TO THE TELEPROMPTER? EVERYTHING'S UPSIDE DOWN...

HEE HEE.

SKIPPY!

WE MADE IT, BRO!

... AND SO GEORGE BUSH HAS SPELLED OUT WHAT HE CALLS "THE VISION THING."

IT IS, LARGELY, A VISION OF MORE OF THE SAME, ONLY WITH FEWER PEOPLE GOING TO JAIL. STILL NO WORD ON WHO'S PAYING FOR IT.

AND NOW, AT THE MOMENT OF GEORGE BUSH'S GREATEST POLITICAL TRIUMPH, HE IS JOINED AT THE PODIUM BY THE ENTIRE BUSH CLAN!

I KICKED **TAIL!** I KICKED **TAIL!**

NEAT SPEECH, DAD!

WASN'T THAT UNCLE SKIPPY?

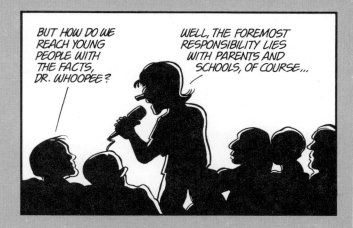

HAVEN'T YOU GOT A CLASS, GIL?

I'M GOING, ED. I JUST CAN'T GET OVER THIS GEOGRAPHY SURVEY...

AMONG 18-TO 24-YEAR-OLDS, U.S. KIDS SCORED DEAD LAST IN GEOGRAPHIC LITERACY. ONE IN SEVEN CAN'T EVEN FIND THEIR OWN COUNTRY ON A MAP!

I'M GOING TO TRY THESE QUESTIONS ON MY CLASS. IF THEY DO AS BADLY AS THEIR PEERS, I'M WORKING TWO WEEKS OF GEOGRAPHY INTO MY COURSE THIS FALL!

GIL, YOU TEACH MATH.

BUT I'M A **TEACHER**, ED! I CAN'T JUST SIT IDLY BY!

BEFORE YOU ALL LEAVE, I'D LIKE A SHOW OF HANDS, PLEASE. HOW MANY OF YOU THINK YOU COULD FIND FRANCE ON A MAP?

FRANCE?

UH...

THAT'S A TOUGH ONE...

HOW ABOUT MEXICO? VIETNAM? THE PACIFIC OCEAN?

UH...

LET'S SEE...

I DON'T BELIEVE THIS! GEOGRAPHY IS ONE OF THE MOST **BASIC** DISCIPLINES!

DISCIPLINE? I THOUGHT IT WAS A "JEOPARDY" CATEGORY.

EVERYONE SIT DOWN.

LADIES AND GENTLEMEN, IF YOU DON'T UNDERSTAND GEOGRAPHIC RELATIONSHIPS, YOU CAN'T UNDERSTAND POLITICS, ECONOMICS OR HISTORY!

IF YOU ARE TO MEET THE CHALLENGES OF THE FUTURE, YOU HAVE TO KNOW WHERE THOSE CHALLENGES ARE COMING FROM! MISS NOURI! WHERE IS KOREA?

UH... KOREA?

YES, KOREA.

IT'S THE PLANET RIGHT AFTER MARS, RIGHT?

IT MIGHT AS WELL BE, YES.

NO, MISS NOURI. KOREA IS NOT BETWEEN MARS AND URANUS...

PLUTO, THEN? I ALWAYS GET THOSE GUYS MIXED UP.

NOT EVEN CLOSE.

HEE, HEE!

HELP ME OUT HERE, GUYS...

YOU DUMMY! KOREA'S NOT EVEN A PLANET!

THANK YOU, MR. SIMMS...

IT'S THE CAPITAL OF AUSTRALIA!

I THOUGHT IT WAS A RESTAURANT. ISN'T IT A CHINESE RESTAURANT?

OKAY, LET'S REGROUP HERE...

MASSACHUSETTS? UH, SURE...THAT'S IN...UH... NEW ENGLAND, RIGHT? NEAR NEW YORK?

GOOD...

WHERE IS IT IN RELATION TO RHODE ISLAND?

HEY, C'MON, MAN. I'M NOT UP ON EVERY RINKY-DINK ISLAND.

MR. SPENCER, RHODE ISLAND IS ONE OF THE 50 STATES!

WHOA, **BIG** MAN WITH HIS TRICK QUESTIONS!

OKAY, LET'S TAKE A BREAK...

OKAY, LAST ONE. WHERE'S NICARAGUA?

UH...

HMM...

THE REASON I ASK IS THAT WE'VE BEEN INVOLVED IN A WAR THERE FOR THE PAST EIGHT YEARS.

OH, RIGHT...

I ONCE READ WHERE NICARAGUA COULD TURN INTO ANOTHER VIETNAM!

WHICH IS WHERE?

UH...

NICE WORK.

NAME-DROPPER.

THE RETURN VOYAGE OF THE "TRUMP PRINCESS" FROM NEW ORLEANS WAS UNEVENTFUL...

MORE CAVIAR TOPSIDES!

AYE, AYE, SIR!

...UNTIL THE FATEFUL MORNING WHEN THE PURSER SPOTTED A FAMILIAR FIGURE LEANING AGAINST THE RADIO MAST.

MY GOD! IT CAN'T BE!

LATER, THE NIGHT MAID CONFIRMED THE SIGHTING.

IT'S...YOU!

THE CAPTAIN WAS DULY NOTIFIED.

SIR? ELVIS IS ON BOARD.

OH, YEAH? BOOK HIM FOR TONIGHT.

IT'S TRUE, SIR. ELVIS IS ON BOARD.

YOU DON'T SAY...

HOW'D HE GET ON BOARD?

WE DON'T KNOW, SIR. HE APPEARS TO BE A STOWAWAY!

WHERE'S HE NOW?

HE'S ON THE POOL DECK, HITTING ON THE TOWEL GIRL.

HEY, BABY! EVER HEAR OF THE KING?

PLEASE.

GOOD TO MEET YA, CAPTAIN...

I KNEW YOU WERE ALIVE, KING. I NEVER GAVE UP HOPE.

I APPRECIATE THAT, MAN. I DON'T KNOW WHAT I WOULD HAVE DONE WITHOUT MY FANS. THEY KEPT ME GOIN'. I COULDN'T HAVE MADE IT WITHOUT 'EM!

SO WHERE HAVE YOU BEEN ALL THESE YEARS, KING?

WELL, BELIEVE IT OR NOT, THEM TABLOID PAPERS ACTUALLY GOT IT RIGHT!

NO! ON A U.F.O.?

THEY HAD LITTLE RICHARD FOR A WHILE, TOO. DID SOME TESTS ON HIM.

TRUMP, NOTIFIED OF ELVIS' PRESENCE ON HIS YACHT, CHOPPERS TO THE "TRUMP PRINCESS" AT ONCE.

I DON'T CARE WHAT IT COSTS! I WANT ELVIS TO PLAY MY ATLANTIC CITY CASINOS!

I HEAR YOU, MR. T!

PUT HIM IN THE DIAMOND SUITE! AND TAKE CARE OF HIM! WHAT ELVIS WANTS, ELVIS GETS!

I'M WAY AHEAD OF YOU, SIR.

AMPHETAMINES, SIR! COMPLIMENTS OF THE CAPTAIN!

Y'ALL ARE GREAT, MAN.

©B Trudeau

TRUMP AND PRESLEY! WE'RE TALKING COMEBACK MAGIC AT THE HOTTEST CASINO VENUE IN THE WORLD! WHAT DO YOU SAY, KING?

DONNY, I WOULDN'T BE HERE IF I DIDN'T BELIEVE IN YOU AS A QUALITY PROMOTER. EVERYTHING ABOUT YOU SCREAMS QUALITY.

THANK YOU.

BUT IT'S GOING TO TAKE MORE THAN $2 MILLION A WEEK, MAN. I'VE GOT A LOT OF RESPONSIBILITIES.

NAME YOUR PRICE, KING! WRITE YOUR OWN TICKET!

I MEAN, I GOT 1,200 ILLEGITIMATE CHILDREN TO SUPPORT.

SAY NO MORE.

WE'VE ALL BEEN THERE, KING. WHAT AGES?

©B Trudeau

... AND I ONLY WANT TO DO THREE SHOWS A WEEK. AND I'M NOT DOING ANY SETS OF MORE THAN 30 MINUTES, OKAY, MAN?

HEY, YOU'RE THE KING.

GOOD, ONE OTHER THING. I ONLY SING JOHN DENVER MATERIAL NOW.

IS THAT A PROBLEM?

WE COULD DROP HIM OVERBOARD. WHO'D KNOW? HE'S DEAD.

©B Trudeau

...AND IN DES MOINES TODAY, THE REVEREND JESSE JACKSON MADE THREE MORE APPEARANCES ON BEHALF OF THE DUKAKIS TICKET.

ROLAND HEDLEY, RECENTLY RETURNED TO ACTIVE DUTY, HAS DETAILS.

ONCE AGAIN, JESSE JACKSON HAS CONFOUNDED EXPECTATIONS, THIS TIME BY CAMPAIGNING VIGOROUSLY FOR A CANDIDATE WHO IS NOT JESSE JACKSON.

WHAT'S IN IT FOR THE FORMER PRESIDENTIAL HOPEFUL? WHAT EXACTLY DID JACKSON GET FROM THE DUKAKIS FORCES IN ATLANTA?

SOURCES WHO WERE PRESENT AT THE TIME HAVE NOW REVEALED TO ABC NEWS WHAT WAS AT THE CORE OF THE JACKSON DEAL...

"YES, FABULOUS PRIZES!"

...AND A GLAMOROUS, NEW DINETTE SET, CHOSEN ESPECIALLY FOR YOU!

JESSE JACKSON! COME ON DOWN AND SIT AT THE BIG TABLE!

LET'S BACK UP A FEW WEEKS.

MR. VICE PRESIDENT, WE'RE REALLY COMING DOWN TO THE WIRE HERE. WE **NEED** A NOMINEE!

IT HAS TO BE SOMEONE I'M COMFORTABLE WITH.

WE NEED A CANDIDATE WHO WILL HELP US WITH WOMEN.

AS LONG AS IT'S NOT DOLE OR KEMP. THOSE GUYS REALLY MAKE ME NERVOUS.

HOW ABOUT SOMEONE WHO'S ACTUALLY STRONG ON WOMEN'S ISSUES?

I WOULDN'T BE COMFORTABLE WITH SOMEONE WHO'S STRONG ON WOMEN'S ISSUES. I'M A TRADITIONALIST.

I'VE GOT IT! SOMEONE **CUTE**!

OKAY, BUT I HAVE TO BE COMFORTABLE WITH HIM.

LOOK, DOLE OR KEMP PROBABLY WOULD HELP THE TICKET, BUT THEY BOTH COME ON TOO STRONG FOR GEORGE.

WHO, THEN?

I DON'T KNOW. BUT THE CHOICE HAS TO BE A BOLD ONE. WE'VE GOT TO DO SOMETHING TO TURN THE POLLS AROUND.

IN THE FINAL ANALYSIS, WE NEED SOMEONE WHO CAN ADD SOME HEFT, SOME BEEF, SOME **WEIGHT** TO THE TICKET!

HI, GUYS! ANYONE FOR GOLF?

NOT NOW, DANNY...

HOW ABOUT PEE-WEE HERMAN?

YOU SURE NOBODY WANTS TO PLAY GOLF?

WE'RE KIND OF BUSY HERE, DANNY... HEY... DANNY!

WHAT ABOUT DANNY, SIR? **HE** SURE AS HECK WOULDN'T OVERSHADOW YOU!

UH... YOU SURE?

WHAT'S GOING ON HERE?

WE'RE PICKING A RUNNING MATE, DAN. GO OVER AND STAND NEXT TO THE VICE PRESIDENT, WOULD YOU?

WOW... EXCITEMENT CITY!

I LIKE HIM, I **LIKE** HIM!

A POLL WAS QUICKLY TAKEN.

MA'AM, WOULD YOU VOTE FOR A CANDIDATE IF HE BORE A FAINT RESEMBLANCE TO ROBERT REDFORD?

ARE YOU NUTS? OF COURSE, I WOULD!

SURE, I'D VOTE FOR HIM. ANYONE THAT GOOD LOOKING MUST STAND FOR REALLY GOOD THINGS.

HE'D SURE HAVE MY VOTE.

YES, IT'S TIME FOR A CHANGE. I THINK MOST WOMEN WANT A REALLY HOT GUY TO BE IN CHARGE OF THE COUNTRY.

THE POLL, ALAS, WAS NOT ADJUSTED FOR SARCASM.

THEY WANT SOMEONE CUTE!

YOU GOT THE JOB, DANO!

OH BOY, OH BOY!

THE BACKGROUND CHECK.

I APOLOGIZE IF SOME OF THESE QUESTIONS SEEM TOO PERSONAL, DAN, BUT I HAVE TO ASK THEM.

I UNDERSTAND. FIRE AWAY!

OKAY, LET'S START WITH YOUR SERVICE RECORD...

I SERVED HONORABLY IN THE NATIONAL GUARD FOR SIX YEARS!

PULL ANY STRINGS TO GET IN?

I DEEPLY RESENT THAT ATTACK ON THE MILLIONS OF MEN AND WOMEN WHO DIDN'T FLEE TO CANADA, AND DAMN SURE DIDN'T BURN THE FLAG!

OKAY, OKAY. EVER BEEN INVOLVED IN ANY KIND OF SCANDAL?

I NEVER LAID A HAND ON HER!

THE BIG DAY.

BUSH IS APPROACHING THE PODIUM NOW, PETER...

AFTER MONTHS OF SPECULATION, WE ARE ABOUT TO LEARN WHO HE HAS SELECTED AS HIS RUNNING MATE...

THANK YOU VERY MUCH. THANK YOU.

I'D LIKE TO BRING SOMEONE UP HERE NOW. LADIES AND GENTLEMEN... THE NEXT VICE PRESIDENT OF THE UNITED STATES!

IT'S...IT'S AN IRISH SETTER, PETER! NO, NO, IT'S SENATOR DAN QUAYLE!

YEA!

SO WHAT'S YOUR BEST ADVICE, PROFESSOR?

A CHANGE OF COURSE, MR. VICE PRESIDENT...

SHIFT THE CAMPAIGN DEBATE AWAY FROM IDEOLOGY AND ISSUES, AND TOWARDS CHARACTER AND COMPETENCE! *THAT'S* A RACE YOU CAN WIN!

REALLY?

SURE! AND FORGET TRYING TO APPEAL TO WOMEN AND MINORITIES! JUST KISS THEM OFF COMPLETELY! AND PLAY UP YOUR BACKGROUND AND EDUCATION! THEY'RE YOUR STRONGEST ASSETS!

GOSH! I ALWAYS THOUGHT SO! SAY, LISTEN, PROFESSOR, HOW'D YOU LIKE TO JOIN MY CAMPAIGN, BE PART OF MY INNER CIRCLE?

WELL, I...

SIR! *NO!*

HUH?

HE'S YOUR EVIL TWIN SKIPPY— *IN DISGUISE!*

WHAT?

DAMN!

GBTrudeau

LADIES AND GENTLEMEN, **TRUMP PRODUCTIONS**, IN ASSOCIATION WITH **DONALD TRUMP PROMOTIONS**...

...IS PROUD TO ANNOUNCE A **DONALD TRUMP** CONCERT-OF-THE-CENTURY TO BE STAGED RIGHT HERE IN THE **TRUMP PLAZA HOTEL AND CASINO**!

AHEM...

OH... FEATURING **ELVIS PRESLEY**!

EVERYTHING'S ALL SET, MR. TRUMP. ELVIS IS PRIMED AND READY TO GO!

GOOD. HAVE ALL THE QUALITY CELEBRITIES ARRIVED?

YES, SIR. TYSON AND DON KING ARE HERE, AND I JUST SEATED SINATRA AND HIS BODYGUARDS UP FRONT.

HOW ABOUT THE VICE PRESIDENT?

HE'S STILL IN HIS DRESSING ROOM. HAVING HIS COSTUME FITTED.

COSTUME?

LET'S SHOW A LITTLE MORE SHOULDER.

"I PLEDGE ALLEGIANCE..."

ON IN **FIVE**, POPPY!

LADIES AND GENTLEMEN, THERE ARE SUPERSTARS AND THERE ARE SUPERSTARS, BUT THERE'S ONLY ONE **SUPERSTAR'S SUPERSTAR**!

LET'S BRING HIM OUT! LADIES AND GENTLEMEN, I GIVE YOU THE **KING** OF ROCK 'N' ROLL, MR. **ELVIS PRESLEY**!

CLAP!

YEA!

CLAP!

CLAP!

THANK YOU! Y'ALL ARE **BEAUTIFUL**! I **LOVE** YOU!

YOU'RE FACING THE WRONG WAY, KING.

THANK YOU! Y'ALL ARE **BEAUTIFUL**! I **LOVE** YOU!

YOU TOOK THEM ALL AT ONCE, DIDN'T YOU?

LADIES AND GENTLEMEN, BEFORE I GET STARTED, I WANT TO BRING OUT A CAT WHO'S NOT AFRAID TO STAND UP FOR OL' GLORY. LADIES AND GENTLEMEN, MR. *GEORGE BUSH!*

THANKS, ELVIS. IT'S GREAT TO BE HERE!

I DIG WHERE THIS CAT IS COMING FROM ON EVERY ISSUE, PEOPLE! PATRIOTISM, GUNS, EVERYTHING BUT DRUGS!

ELVIS, MY PAL NORIEGA FELT THE SAME WAY. IT'S AN *HONEST* DIFFERENCE!

HEY, IS THIS OL' BOY OKAY OR WHAT? LET'S *HEAR* IT, PEOPLE!

I PLEDGE ALLEGIANCE...

SEE, THIS IS WHY I GOT OFF DRUGS. WHO CAN TELL THE DIFFERENCE ANYMORE?

THANK YOU VERY MUCH, LADIES AND GENTLEMEN. IT'S GOOD TO BE BACK.

THE PEOPLE HERE AT TRUMP PLAZA TOLD ME Y'ALL WANTED TO HEAR MY OLD HITS, SONGS LIKE "HEARTBREAK HOTEL" AND "DON'T BE CRUEL..."

BUT I TOLD 'EM, I GOTTA BE ME. TONIGHT I WANNA PLAY SOMETHIN' DIFFERENT FOR Y'ALL. LADIES AND GENTLEMEN, THE MUSIC OF MY GOOD FRIEND, MR. *JOHN DENVER!*

DAMN... DID YOU CALL THE RIOT POLICE?

THEY'RE ON ALERT.

ROCKY MOUNTAIN HIIIGH!

ABC WIDE WORLD OF NEWS.

YEAH, THIS IS ATWATER OVER AT THE BUSH CAMPAIGN...

I JUST WANTED TO LET YOU KNOW OUR TOPIC-OF-THE-DAY IS ENERGY. THE PHOTO OP IS AT AN OFFSHORE OIL RIG, AND THE LINE-OF-THE-DAY IS "READ MY LIPS: TAX BREAKS FOR OIL COMPANIES!"

AND GUESS WHAT? YOU'RE GOING TO PUT IT **ALL** ON THE NEWS TONIGHT BECAUSE YOU'RE PATSIES AND YOU HAVEN'T A **CLUE** HOW TO TELL THE STORY WITHOUT OUR VISUALS AND SOUND BITES! RIGHT?

UH... RIGHT. BUT YOU'RE PUSHING YOUR LUCK, BUDDY!

YEAH, YEAH. BLOW ME A KISS, PUSSY-CAT!

...AND BUSH'S MESSAGE-OF-THE-DAY, DELIVERED IN FRONT OF THIS GORGEOUS VISUAL, WAS, "READ MY LIPS: TAX BREAKS FOR OIL COMPANIES."

IN OTHER NEWS, IN BANGLADESH TODAY...

WAIT A MINUTE! WHAT HAPPENED TO **DUKAKIS'** MESSAGE-OF-THE-DAY? THEY DIDN'T RUN DUKAKIS' MESSAGE-OF-THE-DAY!

FORGET THE MESSAGE! WHAT HAPPENED TO THE NEGATIVE SOUND BITES? HOW ARE WE SUPPOSED TO KEEP SCORE WITHOUT THE DAY'S **NEGATIVE SOUND BITES!**

I WANT MY **N-TV!**

I WANT MY MESSAGE-OF-THE-DAY. I'M CALLING IN.

DUKAKIS CAMPAIGN, MESSAGE CONTROL.

YEAH, I'M CALLING ABOUT YESTERDAY'S MESSAGE-OF-THE-DAY. IT WASN'T ON THE NEWS LAST NIGHT.

YESTERDAY'S MESSAGE? HOLD ON, I'VE GOT IT HERE SOMEPLACE... NO...NO...SORRY, MY OFFICE IS SUCH A...COULD YOU HOLD? I'LL GO LOOK ON THE GOVERNOR'S DESK.

UH, SURE...

FOUND IT! "PICK UP DRY CLEANING AT..." NO, NO, THAT'S NOT IT...

LOOK, WHY DON'T I CALL BACK?

GOVERNOR? THERE'S A GUY ON THE PHONE WHO WANTS TO KNOW WHAT YESTERDAY'S MESSAGE-OF-THE-DAY WAS. ANY IDEA?

SURE...

IT WAS ABOUT MARITIME LAW AND FISHING RIGHTS. I OUTLINED A 23-POINT PROGRAM THAT COULD POSITION THIS COUNTRY TO CAPITALIZE ON ELAPSING PROVISIONS IN EXISTING CHARTERS.

IT INCLUDES ELIMINATING THOSE ANOMALIES ADDRESSED IN THE APPELLATE COURT RULING ON THE STATE OF MASSACHUSETTS v. STAR KIST. IN ADDITION...

"GOOD JOBS AT GOOD WAGES."

OKAY. THANKS.

GOVERNOR, LET ME GIVE IT TO YOU STRAIGHT. YOU'VE GOT TO START DOING A BETTER JOB OF GETTING YOUR MESSAGE OUT THERE!

AND YOU'VE GOT TO LET US HELP YOU, SIR. YOU CAN'T KEEP RUNNING THIS CAMPAIGN ALL BY YOURSELF!

THE FACT IS, THE CAMPAIGN IS GETTING ROUGH. THE SLURS ON YOUR PATRIOTISM, YOUR MENTAL HEALTH, YOUR WIFE, ARE JUST THE BEGINNING!

JOHN, I APPRECIATE YOUR CONCERN...

...BUT IT'S NOTHING I CAN'T HANDLE.

INCOMING!

WHIZZ!

GOVERNOR, I KNOW IT'S NOT YOUR STYLE, BUT IF YOU WANT TO TURN THINGS AROUND IN THE DEBATE TOMORROW, YOU'RE GOING TO HAVE TO FIGHT FIRE WITH FIRE!

SAY HE BRINGS UP THE PLEDGE OF ALLEGIANCE ISSUE. WHAT DO YOU SAY? YOU SAY, "YOU KNOW, NOT SO LONG AGO, PEOPLE WERE BEATEN AND DRIVEN FROM THEIR HOMES FOR REFUSING TO SAY THE PLEDGE ON RELIGIOUS GROUNDS."

"DOES THE VICE PRESIDENT **REALLY** IDENTIFY WITH THAT KIND OF UNTHINKING BIGOTRY?"

I... I CAN'T SAY **THAT**! THAT'S **DIRTY**!

SOMEONE GET ME A MIRROR!

OKAY, OKAY, I'LL SLEEP ON IT.

Panel 1: THE DEBATE HELD FEW SURPRISES... / AS THE SON OF GREEK IMMIGRANTS... / READ MY *LIPS*! MAKE MY *DAY*! EAT QUICHE AND *DIE*!

Panel 2: ...BUT THE PRESS WAS STILL HAVING TROUBLE DIGESTING THE NEW BUSH. / I JUST DON'T GET IT. I'VE FOLLOWED BUSH FOR YEARS. HE USED TO BE SUCH A NICE, DECENT FELLOW...

Panel 3: I KNOW. ALL THE SLURS SEEM SO OUT OF CHARACTER. SOMETIMES I THINK THE GUY WE'RE WATCHING ISN'T REALLY GEORGE BUSH AT ALL!

Panel 4: BINGO. / IT'S ALMOST AS IF HE HAD SOME EVIL TWIN... / YEAH.

Panel 5: ...AND HE'S A CARD-CARRYING MEMBER OF THE *BOUTIQUE ELITE*! / THE "NEW" GEORGE BUSH: PRIME-TIME PIT BULL!

Panel 6: OR IS HE? ABC NEWS, PLAYING A HUNCH, HAS RECENTLY DISCOVERED THAT GEORGE BUSH IS NO LONGER WHAT HE SEEMS TO BE!

Panel 7: IN FACT, THE "NEW" GEORGE BUSH IS NOT GEORGE BUSH AT ALL! HE IS, RATHER, NONE OTHER THAN GEORGE BUSH'S *EVIL TWIN, SKIPPY*!

Panel 8: DAMN! / DON'T WORRY, SKIPPER, THEY CAN'T PROVE IT.

Panel 9: ...AND SOURCES CLOSE TO THE "VICE PRESIDENT" HAVE RELUCTANTLY REVEALED THAT HE IS IN FACT BEING PLAYED NOW BY BUSH'S *EVIL TWIN, SKIPPY*!

Panel 10: APPARENTLY, THE SWITCH WAS MADE IN NEW ORLEANS, SHORTLY AFTER BUSH'S DISASTROUS SELECTION OF DAN QUAYLE AS HIS RUNNING MATE...

Panel 11: SKIPPY WAS INSTALLED IN THE VICE PRESIDENT'S SUITE, AND THE REAL GEORGE BUSH WAS SPIRITED OUT TO THE DEPARTING YACHT OF AN UNIDENTIFIED CAMPAIGN SUPPORTER!

Panel 12: DAMN! HE'S GOTTEN INTO THE LAFITES! / SIR, THE OTHER PASSENGERS ARE STARTING TO SUSPECT. / >HICCUP<

THE REAL **GEORGE BUSH**, SEQUESTERED IN THE WINE CELLAR OF THE "TRUMP PRINCESS," WAS NOT A HAPPY MAN...

IT'S NOT **FAIR!** I SHOULDN'T HAVE AGREED TO THIS!

THIS IS **MY** CAMPAIGN! **I** DID ALL THE WORK! AND NOW MY DARN TWIN IS GETTING ALL THE CREDIT FOR DUKE-BASHING WHILE I LANGUISH IN THIS... THIS FLOATING HOLE!

MEANWHILE, I CAN'T SEE MY FAMILY, I CAN'T TALK TO MY OWN STAFF, I CAN'T EVEN WATCH MY OWN DEBATE ON T.V.!

SIR, YOU'VE HARDLY TOUCHED YOUR YOGURT.

AND TO TOP IT OFF, I MISSED PEARL HARBOR DAY!

HOW COULD THIS HAPPEN, SIR? HOW COULD A MAJOR PRESIDENTIAL CANDIDATE BE REPLACED BY HIS EVIL TWIN?

IT'S BEEN A LONG TIME COMING, MR. DUKE...

FOR MONTHS, MY PEOPLE HAVE BEEN PUSHING ME TO TAKE THE LOW ROAD, TO PLAY DOWN AND DIRTY. BUT IT NEVER WORKED. IT WASN'T ME. I KEPT REVERTING TO THE QUIET, DECENT GUY I WAS RAISED TO BE.

FINALLY, WHEN I PUT THAT STUFF IN MY SPEECH ABOUT WANTING A KINDER, GENTLER NATION, MY STAFF HIT THE ROOF!

AND THAT'S WHEN THEY CANNED YOU?

I TRIED TO EXPLAIN I WAS JUST PANDERING TO WOMEN, BUT NO GO!

WHAT REALLY BURNS ME UP IS I **KNOW** I COULD DO AS WELL AS SKIPPY! YOU THINK RUNNING AGAINST DOLE WAS EASY SLEDDING?

SURE, I MADE A FEW GOOFS, I HIRED A BUNCH OF ANTI-SEMITES, BUT OTHER THAN THAT, I'VE SHOWN **EXCELLENT** POLITICAL INSTINCTS! JUST EXCELLENT! DON'T YOU THINK?

UH... WELL...

WELL, WHAT?

SIR, HAVE YOU EVER TRIED TO SAY "PRESIDENT QUAYLE"? GO AHEAD, TRY.

PRE... PREZ... P-P-PRE... OKAY, WHAT'S YOUR POINT?

...AND THEN A FRIEND OF A FRIEND INTRODUCED ME TO MRS. TRUMP'S PERSONNEL DIRECTOR!

SO EVERYTHING TURNED OUT GREAT, ALTHOUGH FOR A WHILE THERE THINGS LOOKED PRETTY GRIM...

IT TOOK ME A LONG TIME TO GET OVER BEING ATTACKED BY THAT MADMAN WITH A SPATULA. THE POLICE NEVER IDENTIFIED HIM.

IT WAS ME.

WELL, I THOUGHT SO, BUT I COULDN'T FIND YOU IN THE MUG BOOK.

THAT NEW SOCIAL DIRECTOR IS QUITE A DYNAMO, EH, SKIPPER?

THAT'S PUTTING IT MILDLY, JOHNSON.

DO YOU KNOW SHE'S WORKED OUT THEME PARTIES FOR EVERY DAY OF THE WEEK? AND SHE HANDLES ALL THE DETAILS HERSELF! RIGHT NOW SHE'S DOWN BELOW PICKING OUT EACH OF THE WINES...

WHAT?

DAMMIT, JOHNSON, I **TOLD** YOU! NO ONE IS TO GO **NEAR** THAT WINE CELLAR — **NO** ONE!

HAVE YOU THOUGHT ABOUT GOING TO THE POLICE, SIR?

IT'S TOO LATE, MISS. THE DOO-DOO'S TOO DEEP.

THE PROBLEM IS I DON'T TRUST HIM. I DON'T TRUST SKIPPY TO STEP ASIDE AFTER THE ELECTION!

I **KNOW** MY BROTHER! ONCE HE'S HAD A TASTE OF POWER, HE'LL **NEVER** GIVE IT UP! AND WHO WILL BELIEVE I'M THE REAL GEORGE BUSH IF HE DENIES IT?

BUT THAT SHOULD BE EASY TO PROVE, SIR, ALL YOU HAVE TO DO IS COMPARE FINGERPRINTS!

I'M...I'M AFRAID I DON'T HAVE...

OH, GOD, FOOT-IN-MOUTH **CITY!** FORGIVE ME, SIR.

WHAT'S THAT, DADDY?

IT'S CALLED RETIN-A, JEFF. IT'S A CREAM, TO GET RID OF WRINKLES.

ASPIRIN. FOR DADDY'S HEART. HEY... WHERE'S MY HAIR STUFF?...

AND WHAT'S THAT?

JOANIE? DID YOU DROP OFF MY MINOXIDIL PRESCRIPTION AT THE DRUGSTORE? **JOANIE?**

HE'S TURNING 40, MOM. WHAT DO I DO?

LIE. ABOUT EVERYTHING.

DADDY, YOU'VE BEEN ACTING KIND OF FUNNY LATELY...

I HAVE?

WELL, YES, I GUESS I HAVE. IT'S PROBABLY BECAUSE I'M ABOUT TO BE 40. SOMETIMES GROWN-UPS GET FUNNY ABOUT THEIR BIRTHDAYS.

40?

DADDY, YOU **CAN'T** BE 40! SOMEBODY'S PLAYING A TRICK ON YOU! ROBIN HOOD ISN'T 40! EVEN DINOSAURS AREN'T ALLOWED TO BE 40! 40 IS TOO **OLD**!

GREAT.

DAD, DAD, YOU'RE **NOT** 40! THAT'S RIDICULOUS! **MOMMY'S** ONLY 90!

...38...39...**40!** BOY, THAT **IS** A LOT OF YEARS, DAD!

RRING

MAYBE I COUNTED WRONG, 1...2...3...

RRING!

RICK? IT'S LARRY! HOW ABOUT SHOOTING A FEW BASKETS AT THE "Y" TONIGHT?

YEAH?

20... 23...21...

I CAN'T, LARRY. I'M OLD.

OLD? GEE, I'M SORRY.

DAD? ARE YOU DYING SOON?

SO HOW'S OUR NEW BACHELOR MAKING OUT, Z?

NOT WELL, REV...

MIKE'S BEEN DELUGED WITH CALLS FROM ALL SORTS OF STRANGE, EAGER WOMEN. IT'S CONFUSING HIM, CLOUDING HIS JUDGMENT!

WELL, THAT MIGHT NOT BE SO BAD, ZONK. MIKE GOT MARRIED AWFULLY YOUNG...

IT WOULDN'T HURT HIM TO SHOP AROUND A LITTLE, EXPAND HIS HORIZONS.

I DON'T KNOW, REV. TODAY'S DATING ENVIRONMENT IS A LOT DIFFERENT FROM THE ONE MIKE ONCE KNEW!

MIKE, I... I... WANT TO HAVE A BLOOD WORK-UP WITH YOU.

OH, CINDY, ARE YOU SURE WE'RE READY?

"AND I AGREE WITH MR. GEPHARDT'S ASSERTION THAT ASIANS ARE THREATENING OUR ECONOMIC FUTURE..."

"WE CAN SEE IT RIGHT HERE IN OUR OWN SCHOOL. WHO ARE GETTING INTO THE BEST COLLEGES, IN DISPROPORTIONATE NUMBERS? ASIAN KIDS! IT'S NOT FAIR! THANK YOU."

UH... THAT WAS CERTAINLY AN UNUSUAL ESSAY, JENNIFER.

THANK YOU, MR. McGOWAN.

UNFORTUNATELY, IT'S RACIST.

UM... ARE YOU SURE? MY PARENTS HELPED ME.

YOU WANTED TO SEE ME, MR. WHITMAN?

KIM, I JUST WANTED TO TELL YOU HOW PROUD ALL OF US ARE ABOUT YOUR BEING A NATIONAL MERIT SCHOLAR!

IT'S VERY GOOD NEWS FOR THE SCHOOL. IT DEMONSTRATES THAT THE FAILURE OF SO MANY KIDS TO LEARN HERE ISN'T JUST THE SCHOOL'S FAULT. IT REAFFIRMS THE IMPORTANCE OF DISCIPLINE AND PERSONAL MOTIVATION.

YES, SIR. BUT I'M NOT SURE EVERYONE IN THE COMMUNITY SEES IT QUITE THAT WAY.

SHE'S THROWING OFF THE CURVE FOR THE WHOLE SCHOOL!

COULDN'T YOU GET HER TO WATCH MORE T.V.?

HOW DOES YOUR GIRL DO SO WELL, ROSENTHAL? IT'S NOT LIKE SHE GREW UP IN AN ASIAN FAMILY.

NO, BUT WE'VE BEEN RAISING HER LIKE AN ASIAN CHILD.

AHA! LIKE HOW?

BY TEACHING HER THE VALUE OF DISCIPLINE, HARD WORK, AND RESPECT FOR ELDERS.

OH.

BUT DOESN'T THAT GIVE HER AN UNFAIR ADVANTAGE?

YEAH, THIS IS AMERICA, ROSENTHAL!

Panel 1: HOW COULD I HAVE BEEN SIDELINED DURING MY OWN CAMPAIGN? IT'S JUST NOT FAIR! / IN MY EXPERIENCE, LIFE CAN BE LIKE THAT, SIR.

Panel 2: THAT'S EASY TO SAY, BUT YOU DON'T KNOW WHAT IT'S LIKE TO GROW UP WITH AN EVIL TWIN! WHAT I'D GIVE TO SEE MY BROTHER PUT IN HIS PLACE!

Panel 3: HEY, EVERYBODY! SKIPPY BUSH JUST TESTED POSITIVE FOR STEROIDS!

Panel 4: IT'S AMAZING WHAT FALLS OUT OF THE SKY SOMETIMES, ISN'T IT? / YES, SIR. SO OFTEN IT'S SOMETHING FROM A SEAGULL.

Panel 5: "IN KENNEBUNKPORT, MAINE, HUNDREDS OF STUNNED NEIGHBORS TURNED OUT TO CATCH A GLIMPSE OF THE DISGRACED PRESIDENTIAL CANDIDATE."

Panel 6: "IT HAS NOT BEEN A GOOD WEEK FOR THE VICE PRESIDENT. STILL REELING FROM REPORTS THAT THE 'NEW' BUSH WAS IN FACT HIS EVIL TWIN SKIPPY..." / NO COMMENT!

Panel 7: ...THE CAMPAIGN WAS ROCKED FURTHER BY YESTERDAY'S DISCLOSURE THAT FOR THE PAST EIGHT WEEKS, BUSH HAS BEEN TAKING ANABOLIC STEROIDS!

Panel 8: HA! I KNEW IT! I KNEW HE WASN'T THAT TOUGH! / TRY NOT TO GLOAT, SIR. A NATION IS MOURNING.

BUSH ON DRUGS!

Panel 9: DID YOU HAVE ANY IDEA SKIPPY WAS USING STEROIDS, SIR? / NO, BUT I SHOULD HAVE. THE SYMPTOMS WERE ALL THERE...

DAILY NEWS — SAY IT AINT SO, GEORGE

Panel 10: ...THE LOWER PITCH, THE AGGRESSIVENESS, THE OVER-DEVELOPED MESSAGES. IT'S JUST A TRAGEDY. YESTERDAY HE WAS WRAPPED IN OLD GLORY. TODAY HE'S COVERED IN SHAME.

SPORTS / DAILY NEWS / SAY IT AIN'T SO GEORG

Panel 11: WOW...

SPORTS / 0-3

Panel 12: WHO WILL TAKE OVER, SIR? MR. QUAYLE? / HA! HA! HA! HA... NOT THAT HE COULDN'T.

Panel 1:
SIR, WITH YOUR EVIL TWIN DISQUALIFIED FROM RUNNING, WHO'LL TAKE OVER?

ME, OF COURSE! I'M THE ORIGINAL CANDIDATE, REMEMBER?

Panel 2:
OH... RIGHT. ARE YOU SURE YOU'RE UP TO IT, SIR?

UP TO IT? MISS, I HAVE ONE OF THE LONGEST RESUMÉS IN PUBLIC LIFE!

Panel 3:
THAT'S GREAT. ANY SIGNIFICANT ACCOMPLISHMENTS?

I'VE BEEN A CONGRESSMAN, AN AMBASSADOR, A U.N. REPRESENTATIVE, A VICE PRESIDENT, YOU NAME IT!

Panel 4:
THAT'S GREAT. ANY SIGNIFICANT ACCOMPLISHMENTS?

WELL, NOT YET, BUT I'M GOING TO BE THE EDUCATION PRESIDENT.

@BTrudeau

Panel 5:
SIR, BEFORE YOU GO, PLEASE ACCEPT THIS TRUMP TOTE BAG WITH OUR BEST WISHES FOR A SUCCESSFUL RACE!

THANK YOU, MISS...

Panel 6:
YOU KNOW, WHEN I THINK OF THIS COUNTRY AND HOW—WITH OUR 1,000 POINTS OF LIGHT—AND HERE I MEAN OUR TREMENDOUS PREP SCHOOLS AND THIS SORT OF THING...

Panel 7:
...BECAUSE WHEN A PERSON GOES INTO THAT VOTING BOOTH, THEY'LL SAY, HEY, THERE ARE THREE PEOPLE ON OUR TICKET, AND TALK ABOUT JUDGMENT, OR ONE OF THOSE MARVELOUS BOSTON VERBS UP THERE ABOUT... ABOUT... I...

Panel 8:
COME ON, SIR! YOU CAN DO IT! WRESTLE THAT SENTENCE TO THE DECK!

>WHEW!< WHERE'S THE SECRET SERVICE WHEN YOU NEED IT?

Panel 9:
PLEASE THANK MR. TRUMP FOR THE TOTE BAG FOR ME!

I WILL, SIR. HAVE A GOOD TRIP HOME...

Panel 10:
AND REMEMBER, SIR, JUST TRY TO TAKE IT ONE SOUND BITE AT A TIME!

GOOD LUCK WITH YOUR SYNTAX, SIR!

Panel 11:
WOW... WHAT A GREAT GUY! I'M SURE GOING TO MISS HIM, CAPTAIN...

YEAH, ME, TOO.

Panel 12:
AND YET... STRANGELY... I'VE ALREADY FORGOTTEN HIM!

ME, TOO!

WHO?

@BTrudeau

83

1989. A WORST CASE SCENARIO.

...AND WE HAVE DETERMINED THAT THE POISONING WAS CAUSED BY THE INGESTION OF RANCID PORK RINDS!

WELL, PETER, I GUESS THAT'S IT. OUR LONG VIGIL HERE AT BETHESDA NAVAL HOSPITAL HAS COME TO AN END.

IT'S NOW OFFICIAL— PRESIDENT **GEORGE HERBERT WALKER BUSH**, DEAD OF FOOD POISONING AT 65!

GRANDMA! GUESS WHAT?

I HEARD, DEAR. GO FOR IT.

WORST CASE SCENARIO (CONT'D).

GENERAL, WHAT'S OUR MILITARY POSTURE?

FULL ALERT, MR. SECRETARY!

GOOD, JIM, I WANT YOU TO CALL AN EMERGENCY SESSION OF THE SECURITY COUNCIL AT 0100 HOURS.

YES, SIR!

HOW ABOUT THE SOVIETS? HAS THEIR AMBASSADOR BEEN NOTIFIED?

YES. WE'VE ASSURED HIM THAT THERE'S BEEN A SMOOTH TRANSFER OF POWER.

EXCUSE ME! DOES ANYONE KNOW HOW TO MAKE GEORGE'S CHAIR GO UP AND DOWN?

UM... CAN WE HELP YOU WITH THAT LATER, MR. PRESIDENT?

WORST CASE SCENARIO, PART 3.

AND GET SPENCER BACK HERE. WE'RE GOING TO NEED NEW SCRIPTING!

YOU GOT IT.

REMEMBER, NO PRESS EXPOSURE UNTIL HE'S BEEN...

HI, GUYS!

OH, GOOD MORNING, MR. PRESIDENT.

GUESS WHAT? I JUST RAN MY FIRST NATIONAL SECURITY COUNCIL MEETING!

UH... HOW'D IT GO, SIR?

GREAT! I'M HAVING A GOOD HAIR DAY!

RISE AND SHINE, DUCKS! UP AND AT 'EM!

MMPH!

TIME TO WORK THE STREETS! YOU'RE GOING TO MISS THE RUSH HOUR PEDESTRIAN TRAFFIC!

HERE'S YOUR LUNCH BOX. NOW GET GOIN'!

LUNCH BOX? WHAT'S IN IT?

NOTHING, REMEMBER?

OH, RIGHT. I KEEP THINKING WE'RE CAMPERS.

I'M TIRED, ALICE. I'M ALWAYS TIRED...

I KNOW, DUCKS. BUT WE GOTTA EAT. YOU WORK THIS CORNER UNTIL I GET BACK, OKAY?

OKAY... HEY!

WHAT?

GET OFF MY CORNER, LADY! FIND YOUR **OWN** CORNER!

ELMONT! IT'S ME! ALICE! YOUR WIFE!

OH. SORRY. I THOUGHT YOU WERE SOME GORGEOUS HOOKER.

APOLOGY ACCEPTED. HAVE A GOOD DAY.

EXCUSE ME, SIR, YOU GOT ANY SPARE...

I DO, AND I WANT TO GIVE IT TO YOU, BUT WOULD IT BE RIGHT?

SAY WHAT?

HOW DO I KNOW YOU'RE NOT SCAMMING ME? HOW DO I KNOW YOU WON'T SPEND IT ON DRUGS OR WORSE? IN WANTING TO HELP, I COULD, IRONICALLY, ONLY MAKE THINGS WORSE!

OH...YEAH, SEE WHAT YOU MEAN. WELL, WHAT IF I DON'T GIVE YOU A CHOICE, Y'KNOW, THREATEN YOU?

GOOD. I LIKE THAT. THEN **I'M** THE VICTIM, NOT YOU!

OKAY, GIVE ME YOUR MONEY OR I'LL... DAMN! I DON'T SEEM TO BE ARMED!

THAT'S OKAY. I HAVE NO WAY OF KNOWING THAT.

UH-OH... ANOTHER ONE...

GOOD MORNING, SIR!

WOULD YOU HAPPEN TO HAVE A SPARE $18? MY SUBSCRIPTION TO THE "NATIONAL REVIEW" IS ABOUT TO LAPSE!

HEE, HEE! THAT'S NOT A BAD RAP. I'M GOING TO GO FOR IT, YOUNG LADY.

BLESS YOU, SIR. YOU'RE ONE IN A THOUSAND!

THOUSAND WHAT?

POINTS OF LIGHT. I'VE ALREADY MET FOUR OF 'EM TODAY!

HEY! WHO'S THAT?

THAT'S BUSH, DUCKS! WHAT'S HE SAYIN'?

HOW SHOULD I KNOW? THEY GOT THE VOLUME OFF!

I THOUGHT YOU COULD READ LIPS, HON!

OH, THAT'S RIGHT, I CAN. LET'S SEE... HE'S SAYIN'...

..."READ MY... LIPS!"

HMM... MUST BE A LOT OF US OUTSIDE TONIGHT.

OKAY, WHO'S THIS GUY?

THAT'S DUKAKIS. WHAT'S HE SAYING?

WELL, I CAN'T READ HIS LIPS — HE'S TOO TIGHT-MOUTHED, BUT HIS BODY LANGUAGE GIVES HIM AWAY COMPLETELY...

HE'S FUMBLING... HE'S VERY INARTICULATE... APPEARS TO BE MANGLING HIS SENTENCES... BUT HE'S GOT A BIG HEART... AND CONNECTS ON A VERY PERSONAL LEVEL...

AMAZING... HOW CAN YOU TELL THAT?

LOOK AT THE EYES. THE GUY'S A BIG, SLOPPY, EMOTIONAL IRISHMAN!

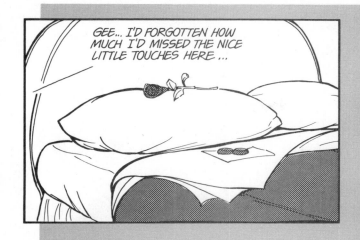

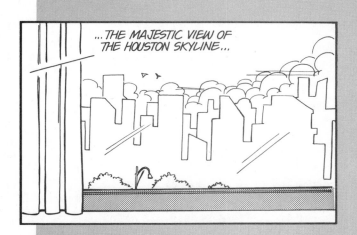

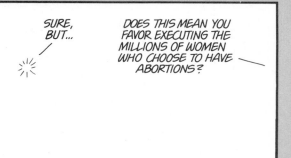

GOOD EVENING. TODAY, IN AN ASTONISHING TURN OF EVENTS, BUSH SCRIPTWRITER PEGGY "POINTS O' LIGHT" NOONAN DECLARED THE ELECTION OFFICIALLY OVER!

PUBLIC REACTION TO NEWS OF THE SHORTENED CAMPAIGN WAS ECSTATIC. THE VICE PRESIDENT, WHILE CLEARLY SURPRISED BY HIS HANDLER'S DECISION, WAS PHILOSOPHICAL WHEN HE MET WITH REPORTERS TODAY.

HEY, IT'S NINE EXTRA DAYS FOR THE TRANSITION. WE CAN USE 'EM. IF IT'S OVER, IT'S OVER, YOU'RE NOT GOING TO CATCH ME WHINING ABOUT IT THE WAY THEY MIGHT UP IN BOSTON!

DUKAKIS, OFF CAMPAIGNING SOMEWHERE, COULD NOT BE FOUND FOR COMMENT.

GOVERNOR DUKAKIS, WE'VE JUST RECEIVED WORD THAT THE CAMPAIGN IS OVER. HOW DO YOU FEEL ABOUT THAT?

WELL, BARBARA, I'LL BE LOOKING INTO THIS MATTER. I'LL BE STUDYING IT. I WANT TO HAVE ALL THE FACTS IN FRONT OF ME SO I CAN ASSESS THE SITUATION.

YES, BUT WHAT ARE YOUR FEELINGS, GOVERNOR? ARE YOU FEELING ANGER? PAIN?

BARBARA, AS THE SON OF GREEK IMMIGRANTS, I FEEL PAIN. WHAT ARE YOU DOING?

UH... I'M JUST TOUCHING YOUR SLEEVE REASSURINGLY.

PLEASE DON'T DO THAT.

WHO'S THAT?

DUKAKIS.

OH... OH, SURE, I REMEMBER HIM...

HE'S GIVING A NEW SPEECH. IT'S ACTUALLY NOT BAD.

YOU'RE RIGHT. BUT WHY'S HE GIVING IT AFTER THE ELECTION?

BEATS ME. HE'S PROBABLY WORKING OFF HIS CAMPAIGN DEBT.

GOOD EVENING. PRESIDENT-APPARENT GEORGE BUSH FLEW TO CALIFORNIA TODAY TO MEET WITH THE CREW OF THE SOVIET ICEBREAKERS THAT RESCUED THE POINT BARROW WHALES.

THE BUSH VISIT WAS QUICKLY FOLLOWED BY THE ANNOUNCEMENT THAT LATER THIS MONTH, DAN QUAYLE WOULD BE MEETING WITH THE WHALES THEMSELVES, AS WELL AS ATTENDING THE FUNERAL OF THEIR DEAD COMRADE.

IN OTHER NEWS, AMERICANS WENT TO THE POLLS TODAY TO MAKE THE BUSH/QUAYLE VICTORY OFFICIAL...

YOU UNDERSTAND THIS IS JUST A FORMALITY.

YEAH, YEAH,

©B Trudeau

MR. BUSH. CAN YOU DISCERN ANY REAL MANDATE IN YOUR VICTORY YESTERDAY?

ABSOLUTELY!

I HAVE A MANDATE TO SAY THE PLEDGE OF ALLEGIANCE, TO NOT JOIN THE ACLU, TO NOT PERMIT MURDERERS OUT ON WEEKEND FURLOUGHS!

I THINK WHAT THE AMERICAN PEOPLE TOLD US IN NO UNCERTAIN TERMS YESTERDAY IS THAT THEY WANT SOMEONE WHO IS **NOT** MICHAEL DUKAKIS!

AND YOU ARE THAT MAN?

IT GETS BACK TO EXPERIENCE. I'VE SPENT A **LIFETIME** NOT BEING SOMEONE!

WHAT SORT OF MAN IS THE NEW PRESIDENT-ELECT? WE ASKED DISTINGUISHED THINK-TANKIST J.S. HAVEL...

WE STILL DON'T KNOW. FOR REASONS BEST GRASPED BY HIS HANDLERS, HE DECLINED TO PUT FORTH A POSITIVE PERSONA.

SINCE HIS CAMPAIGN WAS LARGELY DRIVEN BY NEGATIVE IMAGERY, PEOPLE ARE NOW UNABLE TO THINK OF HIM IN TERMS OTHER THAN WHAT HE IS **NOT**!

PRESIDENT-ELECT UN-DUKAKIS WAS NOT AVAILABLE FOR COMMENT.

©B Trudeau

NAKED AMBITION IS RARELY A PRETTY SIGHT. BUT IN THIS ELECTION'S VICTOR, IT BECAME A GROTESQUE SPECTACLE.

HERE WAS A MAN WHOM EVEN HIS ENEMIES AGREED WAS ONCE THE MODEL OF DECENCY, ENGAGING IN SYSTEMATIC SLANDER IN PURSUIT OF THE PRESIDENCY.

WILL THERE BE SOME TERRIBLE PRICE TO PAY FOR HIS TRANSFORMATION? AS GEORGE HERBERT WALKER UN-DUKAKIS RETURNS TO HIS VICE PRESIDENTIAL DUTIES TODAY, ONLY **HE** KNOWS FOR SURE!

GEORGIE! YOU HAVEN'T BEEN RETURNING MY CALLS, BABE!

HOW'D YOU GET IN HERE?

IN MY CAPACITY AS VICE PRESIDENT-ELECT, I'D LIKE TO SAY A FEW WORDS ABOUT "BONE"...

"BONE" WAS A BRAVE WHALE. HE WAS A WHALE WHO, AS MY GRANDMOTHER MIGHT HAVE PUT IT, COULD HAVE BEEN ANYTHING HE WANTED TO BE. WHAT HE WANTED TO BE WAS ALIVE. UNFORTUNATELY HE'S DEAD.

BUT WE'LL NEVER FORGET THIS WHALE OF A WHALE. WE CARE NOT WHETHER HE WAS A SOVIET WHALE OR AN AMERICAN WHALE. AS WE LOOK DOWN ON HIS CARCASS, WE... WE... UH...

EXCUSE ME. WHERE'S THE DECEASED?

WE ATE HIM.

@B Trudeau

WE'RE BACK, SO STOP FIDDLING WITH THAT DIAL!

MY SADDLEMATE HERE AND I WERE JUST OBSERVING WHAT GENIUSES WE WERE TO PICK BUSH TO WIN LAST TUESDAY. TOMMY, WHEN DID YOU FIRST PREDICT THAT THE NOWHERE MAN WAS GOING SOMEWHERE?

I GUESS IT WAS DURING THE NEW HAMPSHIRE PRIMARY. BUSH STARTED DRIVING TRUCKS ON THE EVENING NEWS, AND DOLE NEVER COUNTER-PROGRAMMED. HOW ABOUT YOURSELF?

IT WAS WHEN BUSH PICKED QUAYLE, THE ONLY CANDIDATE WHO COULD ACTUALLY **ENHANCE** HIS RELATIVE STATURE. IT WAS A MASTER STROKE. THAT'S WHEN I **KNEW** BUSH WOULD GO ON TO TAKE IT ALL!

OF COURSE, IF HE DIDN'T, WE SURE LOOK LIKE JERKS RIGHT NOW.

YEAH, BUT IT'D BE WORTH IT.